TRY VEGAN

Copyright © Malaika Mumba 2020

The author reserves all the right to this book. They do not permit anyone to reproduce or transmit any part of this book through any means or form be it electronic or mechanical. No one has the right to store the information herein in a retrieval system, or to photocopy, record copies, scan parts, etc., without the proper permission of the publisher or author.

Disclaimer

All the information in this is to be used for informational and educational purposes only. The author will not account in any way for any results that stem from the use of the information herein. While conscious and creative attempts have been made to ensure that all information provided herein is as accurate and useful as possible, the author is not legally bound to be responsible for any damage caused by the accuracy as well as use/misuse of this information.

Introduction

Meet me – **Malaika Mumba. Founder of MIMIC Food.**

I am sure we've all heard the hype, "being vegan helped me lose weight", "I feel more alive, energised and happier", "I now have clear smooth skin" and the list goes on and on....

Being a health enthusiast who caters to all lifestyles and wholesome recipes, I decided to compile all my favourite vegan recipes and challenge myself to a 21-day vegan lifestyle. The outcome was exactly how I anticipated it to be:

Week 1:
I lost a lot of water weight. Mainly because of the frequent trips to the bathroom as most of the recipes in this book have a high-water content and are extremely rich in fiber.

Week 2:
I felt a sudden rise in energy levels and my mood changed. It felt like a happy buzz, with higher libido symptoms and clearer focus and concentration.

Week 3:
My skin had drastically improved. I then realised I had no new acne breakouts in the past 2 weeks which lead to a clearer and brighter complexion.

Week 4:
This was an absolute shocker to me, ladies, I had no PMS symptoms!

In this book, you will find:
- 35 nutritious vegan recipes (10 breakfasts, 10 lunches 10 dinners and 5 snacks).
- All meals balanced to ensure one doesn't lose vital nutrients, vitamins, fats and proteins.
- A "how I did it challenge vegan plan".
- A free MIMIC vegan plate meal guide for future reference, to anyone who wants to stick to the lifestyle change after 21 days.

Contents

13 BREAKFAST

1. Berry protein smoothie
2. Vegan breakfast fry-up
3. Chia oats and peanut butter porridge
4. Roasted vegetables on gluten free toast
5. Blueberry and oat pancakes
6. Potato and kidney bean veggie hash
7. Organic crunchy peanut butter on toast with steamed spinach
8. Berry almond butter oats porridge
9. Soy yoghurt parfait
10. 10.Radiance creamy avocado smoothie bowl

24 LUNCH

1. Butternut squash soup and olive oil pan toasted vegan bread
2. Sweet potato and cucumber sandwich
3. Cabbage and lentil stir-fry
4. Gluten free bean and brown rice burrito wrap
5. Lentils with roasted vegetables and cashew nut cream
6. Courgette and lentil bolognese
7. Black bean and brown rice with strawberry and kale salad
8. Raw rainbow salad with beetroot hummus
9. Cabbage filled sandwich
10. Warm lentil and green bean salad

35 DINNER

1. Vermicelli (rice) noodles (gluten free) with mixed peppers
2. Warm lentil and green bean shepherd's pie
3. Roasted tofu and winter vegetables
4. Ratatouille
5. Sweet potato and pomegranate quinoa salad
6. Gluten free chickpea pasta salad
7. Pineapple and green bean butternut squash curry
8. Crispy sweet potato fries with hummus or bean dips
9. Quinoa stuffed mixed peppers
10. Mexican bean rice

47 SNACKS

1. Crunchy veggies with hummus platter
2. Brown rice cakes with peanut butter and soy yoghurt
3. Coconut water sugar free, fruit lollies
4. Popcorn sprinkled with nutritional yeast
5. High fiber, protein muffins

4

First things 1st, who is a Vegan / what is a Vegan diet and understanding the impact of Vegan living.

Who is a vegan?
A vegan, AKA (strict vegetarian), refers to a person who does not consume any food derived from animal products. i.e. meat, dairy, eggs, honey.

The main difference between a vegetarian and a vegan in simple terms is:

Vegetarians: Do not eat animal flesh but may eat animal products, such as eggs and dairy.
Vegans: On the other hand, do not consume anything that is associated with animals.

In other words, veganism is the practice of abstaining from the consumption / use of animal products, particularly in a diet, although "ethical" vegans tend to extend their philosophy beyond food and do so because they are opposed to animal suffering rather than for any dietary reasons.

What is a vegan diet?
A vegan diet / veganism is a type of diet that excludes all animal derived ingredients / products. It mainly consists of a wide variety of nutritious foods such as organic vegetables, whole grains, healthy oils, nuts, legumes, seeds, and fruits.

Understanding the impact of vegan living.
Unfortunately, following a diet based exclusively on plants may put some people at a higher risk of nutrient deficiencies. However, when done right, a vegan diet may result in various health benefits, such as rapid weight loss, lower cholesterol levels, clear skin, blood sugar control etc.

Following a successful vegan diet requires eating a variety of nutrient, dense foods to get the required range of amino acids that are normally derived from animal products. Having knowledge of what makes up a healthy balanced vegan diet, I have ensured all the recipes in this book include all necessary food groups with the right nutrients and minerals your body needs to function. Such as complex carbohydrates, high plant protein foods, healthy fats, vitamins, minerals, fibre and water.

What are you reasons for "trying" the Vegan lifestyle?

There are so many various reasons one would like to "try vegan":
.

For your health:
You now want to improve your health and transition into "clean eating" by improving your diet. This change may lead to clearer skin, less acne, high energy, happier moods and many other benefits.
Also, according to numerous research, vegans are less likely to develop heart disease, cancer, diabetes and high blood pressure than meat eaters.

For the animals:
You may want to take a stand against animal cruelty, maybe because you have an emotional attachment to animals or just believe they have a right to life and freedom. Statistics show that every vegan saves nearly 200 animals per year.

For weight loss:
If shedding some pounds off is on your list of goals, a vegan diet should definitely be part of your plan. Unlike many unhealthy fad diets that leave you feeling tired, hungry and miserable, going vegan provides you with excess energy and generally a happy buzz.

For the environment:
The amount of grain feed required for meat production is a significant contributor to deforestation, habitat loss and species extinction.

All the cool kids are doing it:
Raise your hand if this is your mood right now? I personally, in the past, have been guilty of this one.

So, you've decided that you'd like to "TRY VEGAN", but where / how do you start ?

The idea of eliminating all meat, fish, dairy, eggs etc, from your diet can seem really daunting at the beginning, but usually the idea of a big lifestyle change is a lot scarier than actually doing it.

On the next chapter, I will show you "HOW I DID IT." However, I always advise my fellow foodies to take it slow and go at your own pace.

You can always follow my routine, but bear in mind, any lifestyle change not only takes getting used to but also takes
time to determine what works best for you and what to adapt to.

The most important factor is to "do it right" and If you are contemplating on making this a long-term lifestyle, you need
to ensure all meals include essential nutrients like my recipes do.

For future reference, make sure to take advantage of the free **"MIMIC VEGAN PLATE"** guide for all your meals.

Remember, like most, just because you are "vegan" doesn't mean you are healthy. In future, make sure to avoid all the vegan junk food versions.

How to stay healthy on a balanced vegan diet without losing the nutrients you need.

To be a healthy vegan, one must:
- Eat at least a variety of fruit and vegetables every day.
- Base meals on complex rich carbohydrates like potatoes, brown seeded bread, brown rice, wholegrain pastas etc.
- Have calcium-fortified, dairy-free alternatives such as plant-based drinks and yoghurts.
- Eat various legumes / pulses such as, beans, peas, lentils and other plant proteins.
- Use healthy unsaturated oils and spreads in considerable amounts.
- Drink plenty of still water (roughly between 2-3 litres a day).

Complete my plate.

On the next page, you will find a **"daily nutritional vegan checklist."** Please use this to ensure you are eating enough nutrients to support the vegan lifestyle and also as a guide to know which foods to include on the side to complete some of the recipes.

On the following page you will find a **"MIMIC vegan plate meal guide."** This "plate method" is a brilliant and effective tool that highlights a visual view of how to organize food groups to make sure each meal is nutritionally balanced.

Use this for future reference, to anyone who wants to stick to the lifestyle change after 21 days.

TRY VEGAN

DAILY NUTRITIONAL VEGAN CHECKLIST

TODAY I HAD AT LEAST:

VEGETABLES

- 3 - 5 servings per day
- 1 serving = 1 cup raw or 1/2 cup cooked

FRUITS

- 3 servings per day
- 1 serving = 1/2 cup chopped or whole fruit equals one serving

BERRIES

- 1/2 cup plain

or

- 1/2 cup mixed berries

COMPLEX CARBS

- 3 1/2 cups of whole grains
- 1 serving = 1/2 a cup cooked

or

- 1 piece of wholegrain bread

LEGUMES

- 1 1/2 cups per day

Such as, chickpeas, beans, peas, lentils and other plant proteins

SEEDS / NUTS

- 1 tbsp flaxseeds
- 1 tbsp hemp seeds
- A handful of mixed nuts or 2 tbsp any nut butter

CALCIUM

- Plant-based, calcium-fortified and unsweetened milks and yoghurts
- Blackstrap molasses: In one tbsp, you'll get a gram of protein, plus some iron, calcium etc.

WATER / OILS

- 2 - 3 liters of water
- Meals cooked with healthy oils such as avocado oil, olive oil, coconut oil etc.

THE MIMIC VEGAN GUIDE PLATE

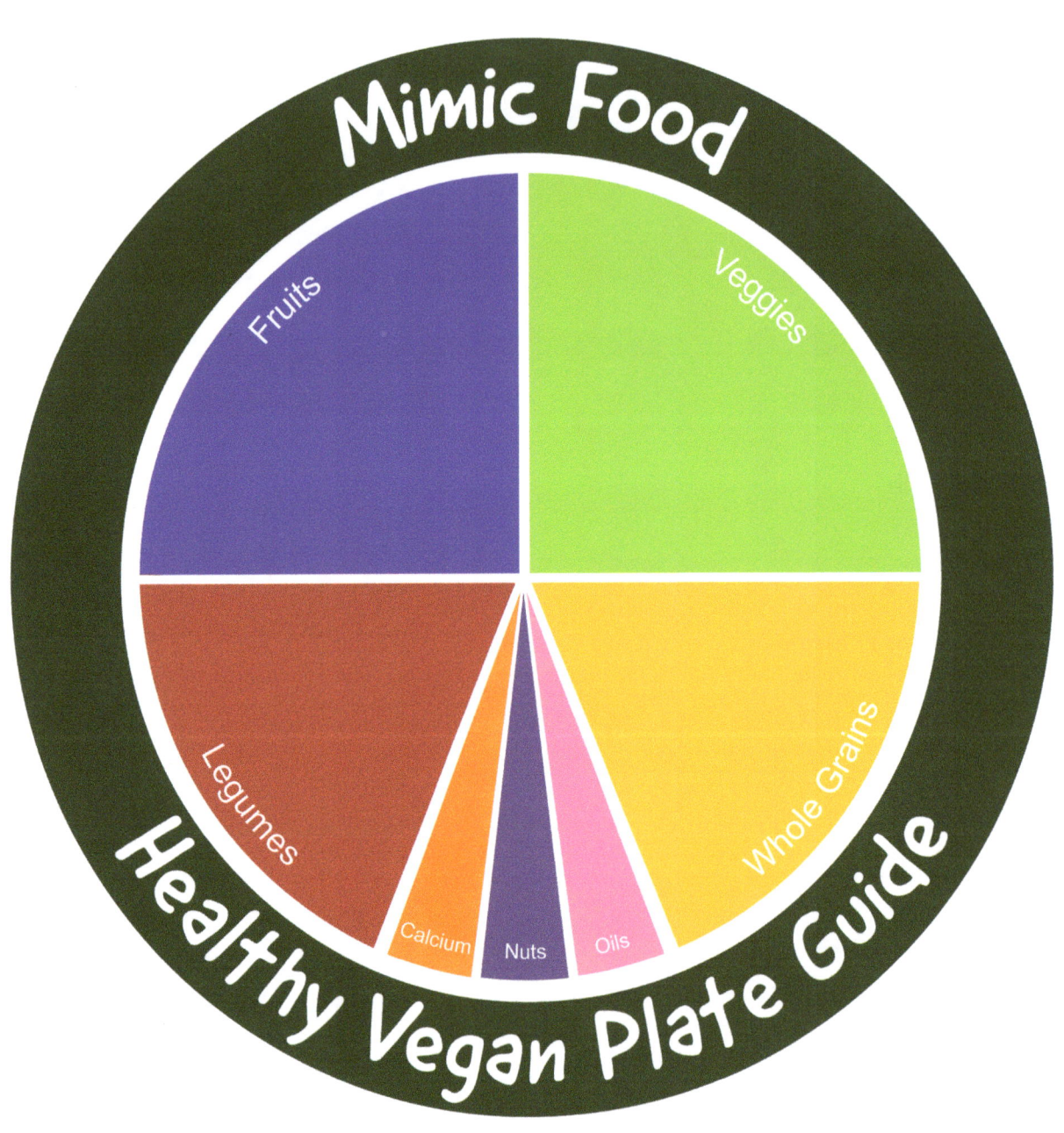

TRY VEGAN

The 21-day challenge plan (how I did it)

I am a huge believer of, "you are what we eat", therefore I always insist on trying to choose foods that are organic, wholegrain, low sugar, gluten-free, have zero / less preservatives etc, basically, foods that are in their natural form.

I would advise that you do the same when shopping for your "TRY VEGAN" ingredients, however I understand if you may need to substitute some ingredients considering you are not able to find them in store i.e breads, pastas etc, as long as your substitutes are still vegan.

Why 21 days?
Have you ever heard of the saying, "it takes 21 days to make or break a habit"? I always follow this principle when trying out something new. After 21 days, it becomes part of you and is easy to stick to going forward.

How I did it.
On the next page, I have shared a daily routine I followed for over 21 days.

Daily routine

On waking:
1litre of room temperature, still water with 2 tbsp of squeezed lemon juice.

After 10 minutes:
Exercise for 30 minutes to 1hr. This was easy for me because I workout from home 5 days a week. A simple cardio routine would be perfect or even "fast walking" around your street.

One hour after water:
Drink the "very berry smoothie". I drank this regardless of what I had for breakfast. It would instantly fill me up. After drinking it, I would go and have my shower, get dressed for the day and then have my breakfast after.
On the other hand, you can drink the smoothie first and follow with breakfast immediately.

Breakfast:
On most diet plans, people are told what to eat on specific days for a certain amount of time. I am not a huge fan of this because you can't really determine people's "on waking" taste buds. Therefore, as all my recipes are nutrient complete, you have the choice of selecting any of the breakfast recipes each morning throughout the 21, day challenge.

Immediately after breakfast:
Take a multivitamin, an omega 3 capsule, a calcium tablet and a B12 supplement.

One to two hours after breakfast:
A cup of any of your favourite herbal teas followed by any of the snacks.

Lunch:
Select any of the nutritious lunch recipes. Start each meal with a piece of fruit.

Immediately after lunch:
Add a tablespoon of blackstrap molasses to 5 tbsp of hot water and drink warm or cold as a dietary supplement. Molasses provide 8% of the daily value for calcium, 10% of magnesium and 20% of the daily value for iron. In addition, they are also rich in B vitamins, particularly B6.

One to two hours after lunch:
A cup of any of your favourite herbal tea's.

Mid-afternoon snack:
Any of the energy boosting snacks with some fresh fruit juice.

Dinner:
Select any of the wholesome dinner recipes. Start each meal with a piece of fruit.

Before Bed:
1 tbsp raw cocoa with hot water and maple syrup (hot chocolate).
This is very important especially whilst on a vegan diet because pure cacao has been found to have anti-inflammatory properties and contains magnesium, calcium, iron, zinc, copper, potassium, and manganese.

TRY VEGAN

Berry Protein Smoothie

Ingredients

- Rice protein powder - 2 tbsp
- Ground flaxseeds - 1 tbsp
- Ground hemp seeds - 1 tbsp
- Any nut butter - 2 tbsp
- Frozen mixed berries - 1 cup
- Banana - 1
- Calcium-fortified, unsweetened almond milk or any of your fortified plant-based milk - 1 cup
- Spirulina powder - 1 tsp (optional)

Method

- Pour milk into blender first
- Add the berries, banana and nut butter
- Then add protein powder, spirulina and seeds last to avoid them sticking to the bottom of the blender
- Blend all ingredients together and If needed, add more milk or still water until you achieve your desired consistency

Vegan Breakfast Fry-Up

Ingredients

- 1 gluten free toast
- 1 tbsp crunchy peanut butter
- Half cup baked beans
- 2 vegan beetroot sausages (made with beetroot, carrot & horseradish)
- Half cup organic tofu
- Handful organic vine tomatoes
- 5 organic chestnut mushrooms
- Sea salt
- 3 tbsp coconut oil
- 1 tsp turmeric powder

Method

- Heat up a pan on medium heat with 1 tbsp coconut oil
- Fry sausages for 10 minutes /until brown (add pinch of salt)
- Clean pan and heat up again with 1 tbsp coconut oil
- Fry tofu for 5-7 minutes on medium heat (add pinch of salt and turmeric)
- Clean pan again and heat up 1 tbsp coconut oil
- Fry mushrooms and tomatoes for 5 minutes (add pinch of salt)
- Heat up baked beans
- To serve, toast and butter the bread

TRY VEGAN

Chia Oats and Peanut Butter Porridge

Ingredients

- Oats - 1 cup
- Chia seeds - 1 tbsp
- Cinnamon - 1 teaspoon
- Crunchy peanut butter - 2 tbsp
- Any plant-based milk - 2 cups
- Coconut sugar or maple syrup - 1/2 tablespoons (optional)

Method

- Put oats into a pot on the cooker
- Add milk, chia seeds, cinnamon and peanut butter
- Over medium heat, stir continuously to combine for 8-10 minutes
- You'll know the oatmeal is done when most of the liquid is absorbed and the oats are thick and fluffy
- Add a splash of milk and coconut sugar or maple syrup on top before serving, if desired

Roasted Vegetables On Gluten Free Toast

Ingredients

- Gluten free bread slices
- Aubergine - half
- Mixed peppers (green, yellow, red) - half each
- Onion - half
- Cherry tomatoes - a handful
- Leeks - half
- Garlic clove - 1
- Sun-dried tomatoes - 3
- Apple - 1
- Mixed herbs - 1 tbsp
- Fresh parsley - 1 tsp

For the cashew nut cream:

- Cashews - handful
- Lemon juice - 2 tbsp
- Olive oil - 2 tbsp
- Nutritional yeast
- Pinch of salt

Method

- Place a non-stick pan on the cooker on medium heat

- Slice and steam the aubergine, mixed peppers, onion, cherry tomatoes, leeks, garlic and sun-dried tomatoes for about 5-10 minutes

For cashew nut cream:
- Toast slices of gluten free bread and spread evenly with cashew nut cream (or reserve to serve on the side)

- Top with vegetables and sprinkle with mixed herbs and fresh parsley

- Serve with apple slices on the side

Blueberry and Oat Pancakes

Ingredients

- Oats - 10 tbsp
- All purpose flour - 1/2 cup
- Baking powder - 2 tsp
- Oat milk - 1 1/2 cups
- Coconut oil - 2 tbsp
- Coconut sugar or brown sugar - 3 tbsp
- Cider vinegar - 1 tbsp (for the pancake fluff)
- Handful of blueberries
- Maple syrup (optional)

Method

- Mix all the dry ingredients (oats, flour, baking powder, sugar) together in a bowl
- Mix all the wet ingredients (milk, 1 tsp oil, vinegar in a separate bowl
- Add the wet ingredients into the dry ingredients and mix until combined. Careful not to overmix the batter or the pancakes will be tough (a few lumps are ok)
- Drizzle the remaining oil onto a non-stick pan
- Pour pancake batter onto the pan to form a circle and immediately place 4-5 blueberries before the batter sets and cook on medium to low heat for about 3 minutes
- Flip and cook for another 3 minutes or so until the pancakes are done
- To serve, top with a handful of fresh berries and maple syrup (optional)

Potato and Kidney Bean Veggie Hash

Ingredients

- Potatoes, washed and cubed - 1 cup
- Canned kidney beans (drained and rinsed) - 1 cup
- Zucchini (washed and chopped) - 1 cup
- Red bell pepper chopped - half
- Mushrooms (sliced) - 1 cup
- Salt and black pepper to taste
- Garlic powder - 1 tsp
- Chili flakes - 1/2 tsp
- Olive oil - 2 tbsp

Method

- Preheat the oven to 150 degrees Celsius
- Season the potatoes with a sprinkle of salt, pepper, olive oil (1 tbsp) and spread out on a baking pan
- Let the potatoes bake for 30 minutes
- In a bowl mix the remaining veggies, beans, olive oil and spices together
- Now place them on top of the potato dish in the oven, stir and continue to bake both for 15 minutes
- Taste and add more salt and pepper if desired

Organic Crunchy Peanut Butter On Toast With Steamed Spinach

Ingredients

- Spinach - a handful
- Chopped tomato - 1
- Sliced banana - 1
- Crunchy peanut butter - 2 tbsp
- Olive oil - 1 tsp
- Wholegrain slice of toast - 2 (gluten free - optional)

Method

- Put the bread slices in a toaster (toast to your preferred level)
- Place toasted slices on a plate and spread with peanut butter evenly
- Place sliced bananas on top of the buttered bread
- Steam the spinach (make sure to not overcook)
- Mix spinach with tomato slices, olive oil and serve

Berry Almond Butter Oats Porridge

Ingredients

- Rolled oats - 1 cup
- Almond butter - 2 tbsp
- Almond milk - 1 cup
- Coconut sugar or maple syrup - 2 tbsp (optional)
- Vanilla extract - 1/2 a tsp
- Mixed blue and raspberries - half cup
- Sliced banana - 1

Method

- Put oats, half the sugar / maple syrup and vanilla into a pot
- Add milk and stir to combine over medium-high heat for 8-10 minutes or until all the liquid has been absorbed
- Be sure to stir the oats several times while cooking to avoid sticking to the bottom
- You'll know the oatmeal is done when all the liquid is absorbed and the oats are thick and fluffy
- Put oats into a bowl and serve with almond butter, the rest of the coconut sugar and top with berries and banana

Soy Yoghurt Parfait

Ingredients

- Gluten free granola - half a cup
- Coconut yoghurt - half a cup
- Mixed berries - handful
- Maple syrup (optional) - 1 tbsp
- Cocoa nibs - 1 tbsp

Method

- Using a medium glass, place half of the yoghurt at the bottom
- Gently put half of the granola on top of the yoghurt
- Sprinkle half of the cocoa nibs on top of the granola and top with half of the mixed berries
- Repeat the above steps with the rest of the ingredients
- To serve, drizzle with maple syrup on the top

Radiance Creamy Avocado Smoothie Bowl

Ingredients

- Sliced kiwi - 1 cup
- Handful of steamed broccoli
- Small avocado - 1
- Plant-based protein powder - 1 tbsp
- Plant-based milk - half cup (+ more to reach desired consistency)
- Spinach or kale - 1 handful

Toppings:

- Fresh raspberries - half cup
- Sliced banana - 1
- Chia seeds - 1 tbsp
- Chopped almonds - 10
- Kiwi - 1

Method

- Combine all ingredients except toppings in a high speed blender and pulse/blend until smooth
- The final consistency should be thick, but slightly pourable when you turn the blender upside down
- If it's too thick, add more almond milk to reach desired consistency
- Transfer mixture to a bowl, top with toppings and serve

LUNCH

Butternut Squash Soup and Olive Oil Pan Toasted Bread

Ingredients

- Red onion - 1
- Carrot - 1
- Garlic cloves - 1
- Celery stick - 1
- Red chilli - 1 tsp - optional
- Rosemary - 1 tsp
- Olive oil - 4 tbsp
- Sage leaves - 1tsp
- Butternut squash - 1 medium size
- Organic vegetable stock - 1 cube with 500 mls water
- Dairy free / vegan gluten free bread - 2 / 3 slices

Method

- Wash and chop the onion, carrot, garlic, celery, chilli
- Heat 2 tablespoons olive oil in a medium to large pot over a medium heat
- Add the sage, rosemary and immediately add the onion, carrot, garlic, celery, chilli, a pinch of sea salt and black pepper, then stir gently for 10 minutes, or until ingredients are soft
- Now halve, deseed and rough chop the squash
- Add the squash and stock to the pot
- Bring to boil and simmer for 30 minutes
- Add salt to tase
- For the bread, slice and drizzle a little olive oil on each side
- Place in a dry, non-stick pan and fry until golden on both sides
- When the squash is tender, pour it into a blender and pulse to a smooth purée – leave it slightly chunky, if you prefer
- Then divide between bowls and serve with the toasted bread slices

Sweet Potato and Cucumber Sandwich

Ingredients

- Sweet potato (fries) oven baked - 2
- Toasted sandwich thins or seeded bread - 4 slices
- Sliced cucumber - half cup
- Sliced tomato - half cup
- Vegan mayonnaise
- For sweet potato fries, you can use the recipe from page 44

Method

- Toast the sandwich thins / bread and set aside
- Spread the thins / bread with evenly layered mayonnaise
- Place cucumber slices on two of the thins / bread and top with potato fries and tomatoes
- Top with remaining two thins / bread

Cabbage and Lentil Stir-Fry

Ingredients

- Green lentils - 1 tin
- White cabbage (shredded) - 1 cup
- White onion (sliced) - 1
- Garlic clove (chopped) - 1
- Olive oil
- Turmeric - 1 tsp
- Vegetable stock cube - 1

Method

- Rinse and drain the lentils
- Heat a pan with the oil on medium heat
- Add the turmeric and fry for a couple of minutes
- Add the onion and garlic and cook for a couple of minutes
- Then add the cabbage and lentils
- Mix the vegetable cube with 1- 2 tbsp of hot water and add it to the stir-fry
- Fry for around 5-6 minutes, or until the cabbage has softened

Gluten Free Bean and Brown Rice Burrito Wrap

Ingredients

- Flour tortillas - 4
- Chopped onion - 1/4 cup
- Olive oil - 2 tsp
- Ground cumin - 1/2 a tsp
- Chili powder / flakes - 1/2 a tsp
- Chopped mixed bell peppers - 1 cup
- Corn and peas mix - 1 cup
- Canned black beans, rinsed and drained - 1 cup
- Cooked brown rice - 1 cup
- Chopped fresh cilantro - 2 tbsp
- Sea salt
- Pepper

Method

- Preheat oven to 150 degrees Celsius
- Wrap tortillas in foil and warm in oven until heated through for about 5-10 minutes
- Meanwhile, combine the onion and oil in large non-stick pan and stir over medium-high heat until onion is golden
- Add cumin and chili powder; stir for a few seconds
- Add peppers, corn, peas and sauté until almost tender for about 5-10 minutes
- Add beans, rice, salt, pepper and bring to simmer for 5-10 minutes
- Remove from heat
- To serve, place warm tortillas on a plate and spoon rice filling equally on each tortilla
- Fold sides of tortillas over filling to form wraps and garnish with cilantro

Lentils With Roasted Vegetables and Cashew Nuts Cream

Ingredients

- Aubergine - half
- Mixed peppers (green , yellow, red) - half each
- Red onion - half
- Cherry tomatoes - handful
- Half a leek
- Garlic clove - 1
- Mixed herbs - 1 tbsp
- Green canned lentils - half a cup
- Sun-dried tomatoes - 3
- Fresh parsley - handful

For cashew nut cream:

- Cashew nuts - handful
- Lemon juice - 2 tbsp
- Olive oil
- Nutritional yeast - 1 tbsp
- Sea salt

Method

- Slice and steam the aubergine, mixed peppers, onions, cherry tomatoes, leeks, garlic and sun-dried tomatoes for about 10 minutes

- Drain the lentils and slightly warm on a pan with some olive oil and add some salt to taste

- Mix the cashews, nutritional yeast, olive oil, lemon, some salt and blend all together until creamy smooth

TRY VEGAN

Courgette and Lentil Bolognese

Ingredients

- Courgettes made into noodles using a spiralizer - 2 large
- Onion (washed and diced - 1 medium
- Garlic clove (washed and minced) - 1
- Carrot (washed and diced) - 1 large
- Chestnut mushrooms (washed and finely diced) - 1 cup
- Cooked lentils (drained) - 1 cup
- Tomatoes (washed and chopped) - 2
- Fresh basil (washed and chopped) - 1tbsp
- Vegetable stock - 1 cube
- Salt and pepper to taste
- Olive oil

Method

- Drizzle olive oil in a saucepan
- On medium heat, fry the onions, garlic and carrots until softened
- Add the tomatoes, mushrooms, lentils, vegetable cube, a pinch of sea salt and pepper and herbs
- Cook until vegetables begin to shrink and thicken
- Meanwhile, tip your courgettes into a separate pan with 1 tbsp olive oil, a pinch of salt and a splash of water
- Heat for 5-8 minutes or until softened but don't overcook or they will turn mushy
- Now add them to your serving bowls and top with the vegetable bolognese

Black Bean and Brown Rice with Strawberry and Kale Salad

Ingredients

- Kale leaves - 3-5 leaves (stems removed)
- Almonds - half a cup
- Olive oil - 2 tbsp
- Garlic cloves - 1
- Powdered ginger - half a tsp
- Salt and pepper, to taste
- Strawberries sliced - 1 cup
- Ingredients for Mexican black bean rice on page 46

Method

- For Mexican black bean rice, see page 46
- For kale salad, wash the kale leaves and slice into small, bite-sized pieces. Set aside
- In a frying pan over low heat, toast the almonds. Stir continuously to avoid burning, and remove from the pan immediately once toasted (5-8 minutes). Set aside
- Mince the garlic and add to the pan with the olive oil over low heat. Simmer for 1 minute or until the garlic is golden
- Add the ginger, salt, and pepper to the pan and stir. Now add the kale to the frying pan and cook until veggies soften
- Place the kale in a salad bowl to cool slightly, add the almonds, strawberries and toss to combine
- Serve salad with hot rice on the side

Raw Rainbow Salad With Beetroot Hummus

Ingredients

- Courgette - handful
- Carrots - 2
- Vine tomatoes - handful
- Broccoli - handful
- Sugar snap peas - handful
- Yellow pepper - handful
- Pumpkin seeds - 1 tbsp

(slightly steam the vegetables if not used to raw food)

For the hummus:
- Beetroots - 2
- Cooked chickpeas rinsed and drained - 1 can
- Lemon juice - 1
- Salt and black pepper to taste
- Garlic clove - 1
- Tahini - 2 tbsp
- Virgin olive oil

Method

For beetroot hummus:
- Preheat oven to 160 degrees Celsius
- Wash the beetroot, peel / cut off any stems, wrap in foil, drizzle on a bit of olive oil, place in the oven and roast for a hour or until soft
- When done, place in a small bowl / cup in the fridge
- Once your beetroot is cooled, cut into pieces and place it in your food processor
- Add chickpeas, lemon juice, garlic, tahini, salt, and blend until smooth
- Place in a bowl / cup and drizzle olive oil and mix
- Taste and adjust seasonings as needed, adding more salt, lemon juice, or olive oil if needed
- If it's too thick, add a bit of water
- For raw salad, wash and slice or spiralize vegetables
- Serve salad on a plate with beetroot hummus and sprinkle with pumpkin seeds

Cabbage Filled Sandwich

Ingredients

- Cabbage filling recipe (page 27)
- Soy egg-free mayonnaise or any vegan mayonnaise
- Tomato (sliced) - 1
- Vegan wholegrain bread (toasted - 2 slices

Method

- If using leftovers from cabbage and lentil stir-fry (page 27), slightly warm the mixture
- Toast the slices of bread and set aside
- Spread the bread with evenly layered mayonnaise to your preference
- Place cabbage on one slice and top with the slices of tomato
- Enjoy with some fruit juice

Warm Lentil and Green Bean Salad

Ingredients

- Organic green lentils (rinsed and drained) - 1 tin
- Green beans - 1 cup
- Olive oil
- Red onion (peeled and chopped) - 1
- Mixed frozen peas and sweetcorn - 1 cup
- Chopped carrots - half cup
- Clove of garlic - 1
- Vegetable stock - 1 cube
- Mixed herbs spice - 1 tsp
- Sea salt

Method

- Wash and trim the green beans, then cut into pieces
- In a pot, bring water to a boil, then drop in the green beans to blanch them for 3 minutes (or longer, but I like mine bright green and still crunchy
- Then strain the green beans through a colander and rinse under cold running water to stop them from cooking
- Heat a non-stick pan on low / medium heat and pour oil
- Fry the onions and garlic for less than a minute and add the carrots, green beans and frozen veg. Cook for 1 more minute
- Add the lentils and stock cube (mixed with 4 tablespoons hot water)
- Now add salt and the mixed herb spice
- Stir and cover the pan and turn off the cooker
- Serve and enjoy!

DINNER

Vermicelli (rice) Noodles (gluten free) with Mixed Peppers and Black Beans

Ingredients

- Vegan rice noodles broken into pieces - 2 cups
- Canned black beans (washed and drained) - 1 tin
- Grated carrots - 1/2 a cup
- Thinly sliced and washed mixed peppers - 1cup
- Brown onion (washed and sliced) - 1 small
- Garlic clove (minced) - 1
- Low-sodium soy sauce - 1tbsp
- Chili flakes - 1tsp
- Vegetable cube - 1
- Olive oil

Method

- Bring 3 cups water to a boil in medium saucepan and add broken noodles
- Cover and remove from heat and let sit for 5 to 7 minutes
- Drain and discard water
- Meanwhile, whisk together soy sauce, chilli flakes, vegetable cube and 1/4 cup hot water in small bowl
- Drizzle olive oil in a non-stick pan over medium-high heat
- Add onion, garlic and stir-fry 1 minute
- Now add the peppers and beans, and cook for a couple of minutes
- Add soy sauce mixture, continue stirring and cook 1 minute more or until peppers are tender
- Now stir in the drained noodles
- Add more salt and pepper to taste
- Serve and enjoy

Warm Lentil & Green Bean Shepherd's Pie

Ingredients

- Medium onion (diced) - 1
- Cloves garlic (minced) - 2
- Cooked green lentils (rinsed and drained) - 1 tin
- Vegetable stock - 1/4 cup mix
- Fresh thyme - 2 tbsp
- Green beans (trimmed and cut) - 1/2 cup
- Mixed frozen veggies - 1 cup
- Olive oil

For mashed potatoes:
- Potatoes (thoroughly washed). Quantity will depend on your baking dish
- Vegan butter - 2-3 tbsp
- Salt and pepper (to taste)
- Chilli flakes - 1 tsp (optional)

Method: Mashed potatoes

- Slice the potatoes in half, place in a large pot and fill with water until they're just covered
- Bring to a low boil on medium-high heat, add salt, cover and cook for 20-30 minutes or until they slide off a knife very easily
- While potatoes are cooking, preheat oven to 200 degrees Celsius and lightly grease and place your baking dish in the oven
- Once potatoes are cooked, drain, add back to the pot to evaporate any remaining water, then transfer to a mixing bowl
- Use a masher or large fork to mash until smooth. Add desired amount of vegan butter and season with salt, pepper and chilli flakes to taste
- Cover and set aside

Warm Lentil & Green Bean Shepherd's Pie

Method: Filling

- In a large pan over low / medium heat, drizzle some olive oil
- Sauté the onions and garlic until lightly browned
- Add a pinch each of salt and pepper then add the lentils, stock, thyme
- Stir-fry consitently
- Now add the frozen veggies and green beans and cook for 5-10 minutes
- Taste and add extra seasonings if needed
- Then transfer to your greased baking dish and carefully top with mashed potatoes
- Smooth down with a spoon or fork and season with another pinch of pepper and a little sea salt
- Place on a baking sheet / foil to catch overflow
- Bake for 10-15 minutes or until the mashed potatoes are lightly browned on top
- Allow to cool briefly before serving
- You can store the rest in the fridge for up to a few days

Roasted Tofu and Winter Vegetables

Ingredients

- Extra, firm tofu (drained and cut into cubes) - handful
- White baby potatoes - handful
- Garlic clove (peeled) - 1
- Courgette (washed and cubed) - 1 medium
- Chestnut mushrooms (washed) - 1 cup
- Cherry tomatoes (washed) - handful
- Mixed herbs - 1tbsp
- Chilli flakes (optional) - 1 tsp
- Salt and pepper to taste
- Olive oil

Method

- Preheat oven to 150 degrees Celsius
- Place tofu on a baking sheet or tray, drizzle with olive oil and season with salt and pepper (mix well)
- Put the tofu in the oven and, in a mixing bowl, add all remaining vegetables
- Now season with the mixed herbs, a pinch of sea salt and pepper and drizzle with olive oil. Make sure all vegetables are evenly coated
- Remove the tofu tray / sheet and place the seasoned vegetables on the tray and mix vegetables together
- Add more oil or seasoning if needed
- Roast for 30 minutes and serve

Ratatouille

Ingredients

- Tomatoes (washed and blended) - 2 cups
- Zucchini (washed and sliced) - 1 large
- Eggplant (washed and sliced) - 1 large
- Medium red tomatoes (washed and sliced) - 3
- Extra-virgin olive oil
- Apple cider vinegar - 1tsp
- Minced garlic - 1tsp
- Fresh basil (chopped) - handful
- Mixed herbs - 1tsp
- Sea salt and pepper to taste
- Chili flakes - optional
- Red onion (sliced) - 2

Method

- Preheat the oven to 180 degrees Celsius and lightly grease a baking dish and set aside
- In a medium mixing bowl, combine the blended tomatoes, drizzle oil, and vinegar
- Stir in the garlic, basil, herbs, salt, pepper and chili flakes
- Pour the tomato mixture into the prepared baking dish and smooth it into an even layer on the bottom of the pan
- Stack the vegetable slices in alternating patterns (e.g. onion, zucchini, eggplant, tomato; repeat) and place them on their side in the pan, leaning against the edge of the pan
- Repeat until you've formed a couple of rows of vegetables, filled the pan, and used up all of the slices
- Bake for about an hour, until the tomato sauce at the bottom is bubbling and the vegetables are tender
- Sprinkle some chopped fresh basil before serving (optional). Serve hot or cold

Sweet Potato and Pomegranate Quinoa Salad

Ingredients

- Sweet potato (washed, peeled, and diced) - 1 large
- Cooked quinoa - 1 cup
- Rocket leaves (washed and drained) - 2 cups
- Red onion (washed and sliced) - 1 small
- Pomegranate seeds - 1
- Olive oil

For the dressing:

- Olive oil - 1 tbsp
- Apple cider vinegar - 1 tsp
- Salt & pepper to taste

Method

- Preheat oven to 200 degrees Celsius
- In a bowl, place the sweet potato, drizzle with olive oil, season with salt and pepper and mix
- Lay on a baking sheet and bake for 30 minutes or until potatoes are done
- In a serving bowl, mix together pomegranate seeds, onion, cooked quinoa, and toss with the dressing
- Once sweet potato has baked and cooled down, add to the salad bowl and mix
- Serve and enjoy

Gluten Free Chickpea Pasta Salad

Ingredients

- Gluten free brown rice pasta (available on healthy brands) - 1 cup
- Red onion - 1
- Large cucumber - 1
- Cherry tomatoes - handful
- Cooked chickpeas - 1 tin
- Black olives - half a cup
- Sunflower seeds - 2 tbsp
- Fresh parsley - handful

For the dressing:
- Juice from 1 lemon
- Apple cider vinegar - 1tbsp
- Olive oil - 1tbsp
- Garlic clove (minced) - 1
- Chilli flakes - 1tsp
- Salt and pepper (pinch)

Method

- Cook the pasta as per the packet instructions

- Toast the sunflower seeds (fry on dry pan or bake for a couple of minutes)

- Wash and slice the red onion, dice the cucumber, halve the cherry tomatoes, drain and rinse the chickpeas, chop the parsley and halve the olives

- Now add all these ingredients into a mixing bowl, along with the toasted sunflower seeds

- Prepare the dressing by mixing all the ingredients together in a small bow

- Drain the pasta and run cold water through it, then transfer to the mixing bowl and pour the dressing on top

- Stir the pasta salad to combine and serve

Pineapple and Green Bean Butternut Squash Curry

Ingredients

- Butternut squash (peeled and cut into chunks) - 1 medium
- Green beans (washed, trimmed and cut) - 1 cup
- Pineapple (peeled and cut in same chunks size as squash) - 1/2
- Parsley or coriander leaves (washed and chopped) - handful
- Brown onion (washed and sliced) - 1
- Turmeric powder - 1 tbsp
- Coconut milk - 1 small tin
- Vegetable stock - 1 cube
- Sea salt and pepper
- Olive oil

Method

- Drizzle and heat the oil in a pan on medium heat and fry the onion for 2 minutes or until softened
- Stir in the turmeric powder, a pinch of sea salt and pepper
- Then add the squash, coconut milk, 1 cup of water, vegetable stock and stir and simmer
- After 10 mins cooking, tip in the green beans
- Stir and simmer again for another 15-20 minutes or until squash is tender
- Taste and add more seasoning if needed Bend now add the pineapple and parsley and cook for just a few minutes
- Serve in bowls while hot

TRY VEGAN

Crispy Sweet Potato Fries with Hummus or Bean Dips

Ingredients

- Sweet potatoes - 3
- Cornstarch - 1 tsp
- Tomatoes - 2
- Olive oil
- Sea salt
- Black pepper
- Chilli flakes - 1 tsp
- Hummus - half a cup
- Any bean dip of your choice - 1/2 cup

Method

- Preheat the oven to 150 degrees Celsius
- Peel the sweet potatoes (optional), (I always leave the skins on) and cut them into fry-shaped pieces
- Toss the uncooked fries into a mixing bowl and sprinkle with cornstarch (if using) and drizzle the olive oil
- Season with salt, pepper, and spices of your choice (I used chilli flakes)
- Mix to distribute evenly
- Arrange your fries in a single layer on a baking tray and don't overcrowd, otherwise they will not crisp up
- Bake for 20 minutes, then flip the fries so they can cook on all sides and bake for another 20 minutes or until crispy
- Slice the tomatos and serve with the hummus and bean dips

Quinoa Stuffed Mixed Peppers

Ingredients

- Uncooked quinoa (rinsed and drained) - 1 cup
- Frozen peas and sweetcorn mix - 1 cup
- Black beans (rinsed and drained) - 1 tin
- Mixed whole peppers (red, green, yellow) - 4-6
- Small onion (washed and diced) - 1
- Garlic cloves (minced) - 1
- Vegetable stock cube - 1
- Water - 2 cups
- Olive oil

Method

- Preheat oven to 150 degrees Celsius and line a deep baking dish with baking paper
- Mix quinoa, water, vegetable cube together in a saucepan and bring to a boil
- Cover, reduce heat and simmer until quinoa is tender and water is absorbed (about 15 minutes)
- Drizzle and heat olive oil in a large pan over medium heat
- Fry and stir onion and garlic until slighthly golden
- Add peas, sweetcorn, beans and cook until slightly tender (3 to 5 minutes)
- Stir quinoa into vegetable mixture and season with salt and pepper to taste
- Cut the top of the peppers off (as per picture)
- Now fill the cut bell peppers with the quinoa-vegetable mixture and place them in the prepared baking dish
- Cover the dish with aluminium foil
- Bake in the preheated oven until bell peppers are slightly tender, about 15-20 minutes
- Remove aluminium foil cover and drizzle some olive oil and salt over the peppers and continue to bake until peppers are done
- Remove from oven and allow to cool and serve

Mexican Bean Rice

Ingredients

- Red onion (washed and sliced) - 1 small
- Cooked brown rice - 1 cup
- Cooked canned kidney beans (rinsed and drained - 1 cup
- Chopped mixed bell peppers - 1 cup
- Frozen corn - 1/2 cup
- Ground cumin - 1tsp
- Fresh cilantro (chopped) - 2 tbsp
- Chili powder / flakes - 1/2 tsp
- Olive oil
- Lemon juice (optional) - 1/2 a tsp

Method

- Combine the onion and oil in large non-stick pan and stir over medium-high heat until onion is golden
- Add cumin, chili powder and stir for less than a minute
- Add peppers, corn and sauté until almost tender (about 5 minutes) or less
- Add drained beans, cooked rice and continue stirring (drizzle more oil if needed)
- Season with salt and pepper to taste
- Remove from heat, serve on a plate and squeeze lemon juice if desired

SNACKS

Crunchy Veggies With Hummus Platter

Ingredients

- Cucumber - half
- Carrots - 2
- Celery stalks - 2
- Mixed peppers - 2
- Hummus - 1 cup
- Lemon juice - 1 lemon
- Pitta bread / slices

Method

- Wash and slice all vegetables
- Place / spread all vegetables on a plate
- Mix hummus with lemon juice
- Serve with pita breads

Brown Rice Cakes With Peanut Butter and Soy Yoghurt

Ingredients

- Crunchy peanut butter - 1 tbsp
- Multigrain or brown rice cakes - 2
- Soy yoghurt - 1/2 cup
- Banana - 1

Method

- Spread peanut butter on one rice cake
- Spread yoghurt on other rice cake
- Top each cake with sliced bananas

Coconut Water Sugar-Free Fruit Lollies

Ingredients

Needed - ice lolly trays

Quantity of the below ingredients will depend on the size of your lolly trays

- Coconut water
- Maple syrup (optional)
- Mango's
- Kiwis
- Blueberries
- Strawrberries

Method

- Wash / slice all fruits

- Mix the coconut water with the maple syrup (optional)

- Fill your ice lolly trays with fruit in the following order: blueberries, kiwis, strawberries and mango's

- Pour coconut water until trays are full

- Carefully add a lolly stick to each tray, make sure not to mash the fruits

- Add the lid, then pop the ice lolly mould into the freezer until completely frozen

- This may take a couple of hours or overnight, depending on your freezer

Popcorn Sprinkled With Nutritional Yeast

Ingredients

- White popcorn kernels
- Extra-virgin olive oil
- Sea salt
- Nutritional yeast

Method

- Air pop the corn kernels

- Spill the popcorn into a large bowl

- Drizzle with olive oil, enough to lightly coat

- Sprinkle with salt to your own taste

- Generously sprinkle with nutritional yeast

- Toss and serve

High Fiber Protein Muffins

Ingredients

Needed - muffin tin

- Rolled oats (gluten free) - 1 cup
- Bananas (mashed) - 1 cup
- Plant-based protein powder (I used rice protein) - 4 tbsp
- Flaxseed and chia seed mix - 4 tbsp
- Baking powder - 1 tsp
- Mixed sunflower and pumpkin seeds - 2 tbsp
- Plant-based milk of choice - 1 cup
- Coconut oil - 2 tbsp
- Coconut sugar or maple syrup - 4 tbsp

Method

- Preheat oven to 150 degrees Celsius
- Grease a 12 muffin tin with a little oil and place in the oven
- Using a blender, turn the rolled oats into flour
- In a large mixing bowl, combine all the dry ingredients
- Warm the coconut oil on medium heat in a pan and add the mashed banana and the milk
- Add the coconut sugar or maple syrup and whisk until evenly combined
- Cautiously add the liquid mixture into the dry ingredients and stir until all ingredients are combined
- Pour the mixture evenly into the muffin tins
- Transfer to the oven and bake for 20-25 minutes or until a toothpick inserted in the centre comes out clean
- Please note, baking time will vary for every oven

TRY VEGAN

Author's Note

Writing a cookbook is harder than I thought and more rewarding than I could have ever imagined!

After one-plus years of recipe testing, manuscript writing, photo shoots, proofreading, and endless dishwashing, I'm beyond thrilled to finally share my favourite vegan recipes with the world.

None of this would have been possible without some of my loved ones who stood by me during every picture selection struggle and all other successes. I am also grateful to my mother for the continuous encouragement, as well as to my publishers for bringing my recipes to life.
Above all, I am grateful to GOD and excited to see what he said he would do manifest.

TRY VEGAN

www.ingramcontent.com/pod-product-compliance
Lightning Source LLC
Chambersburg PA
CBHW061056170426
43192CB00023B/2892